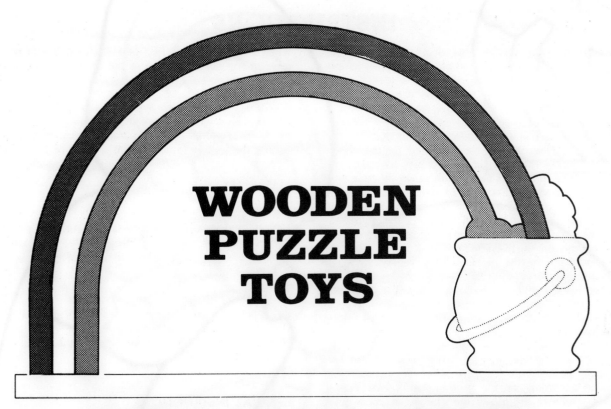

WOODEN PUZZLE TOYS

Patterns and Instructions for 24 Easy-to-Do Projects

Ed Sibbett, Jr.

DOVER PUBLICATIONS, INC.
New York

INSTRUCTIONS

Old-fashioned wooden toys of all types have had perennial appeal to young and old alike, but the simple wooden puzzle toy has always been a special timeless favorite. Long after the racing cars, the plastic boats and the metal robots have lost their charm, a wooden puzzle toy will still be enjoyed.

This book contains patterns and instructions for making the twenty-four toys pictured on the covers of this book. They are simple and easy to make, and you will be proud to hand them down to your children and grandchildren. The patterns for the toys are printed on special paper with transfer ink so that the heat from a home iron will transfer the design onto wood, eliminating the trouble of tracing patterns. The dark lines on the patterns are the cutting lines; the dotted lines are the painting lines. Where the combination of dotted and dark lines might be confusing, there is an additional small drawing which shows the cutting lines only. These small drawings also serve as "test patterns" for determining the correct heat setting for your iron.

The puzzle toys made from plates 3, 4, 5, 6, 9, 10, 15, 21 and 24 are intended to be hung. These toys should be cut from ½" pine. After the toy has been made according to the general instructions below, drill a hole in the top of the toy and attach a piece of heavy cord or a leather thong.

The puzzle toys made from plates 13 and 22 are intended to fit on a dowel which goes through the toy into a base. The transfer pattern indicates where the dowel fits. Use a ¼" or ⅛" round dowel and a wood base made from ¾" pine shelving. Drill a hole through the completed toy in the appropriate spot to receive the dowel. The flowers on plate 20 should be attached to dowels, and the dowels set into a flower pot. The rainbow and the pot of gold on plate 23 stand on a wooden base, which appears as part of the transfer pattern. Use the transfer as a model for cutting the base, and cut it from a piece of 2" wood.

MATERIALS

½" or ¾" pine shelving
Table-mounted hobby or scroll saw. (Hand-held power saws will not give satisfactory results, but skilled craftsmen may be able to cut some of the projects with a coping saw.)
Iron
Medium-fine sandpaper
Paints (acrylics, poster paints, etc.) or marking pens
Dowels (for plates 13, 20 and 22)
Heavy cord or leather thongs (for plates 3, 4, 5, 6, 9, 10, 15, 21 and 24)
Drill

GENERAL INSTRUCTIONS

1. Select a piece of wood that is free from knots or blemishes, and gently sand the surface so that it is smooth. The entire toy must be cut from one piece of wood. Note that all hanging toys must be cut from

Instructions continue after patterns.

Published in Canada by General Publishing Company, Ltd., 30 Lesmill Road, Don Mills, Toronto, Ontario.
Published in the United Kingdom by Constable and Company, Ltd.

Wooden Puzzle Toys. Patterns and Instructions for 24 Easy-to-Do Projects is a new work, first published by Dover Publications, Inc., in 1978.

International Standard Book Number: 0-486-23713-3
Library of Congress Catalog Card Number: 78-56744

Manufactured in the United States of America
Dover Publications, Inc.
31 East 2nd Street
Mineola N.Y. 11501

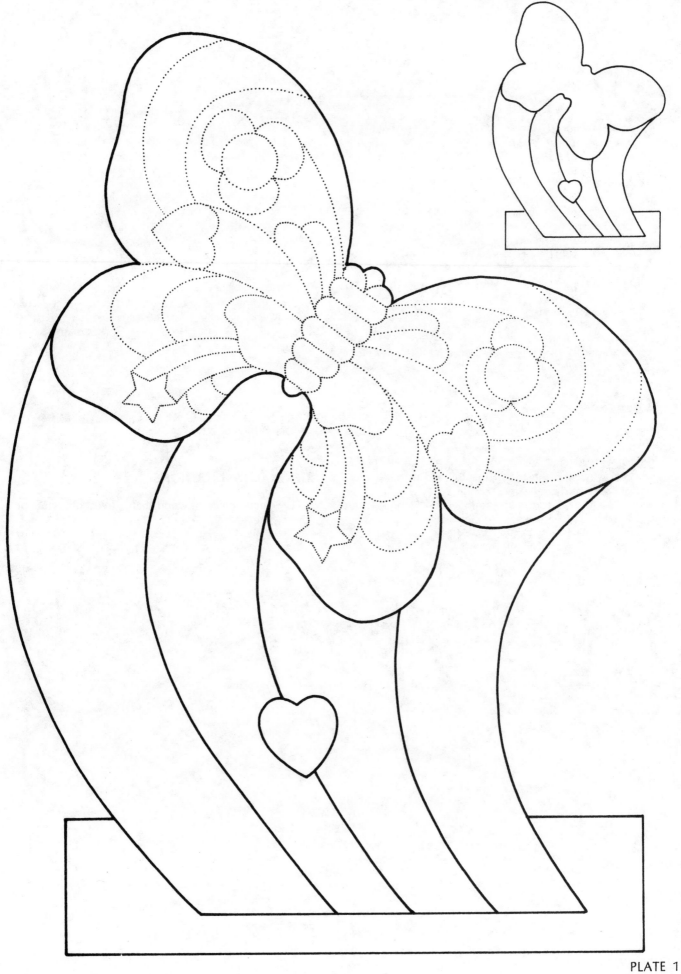

PLATE 1

PLATE 4

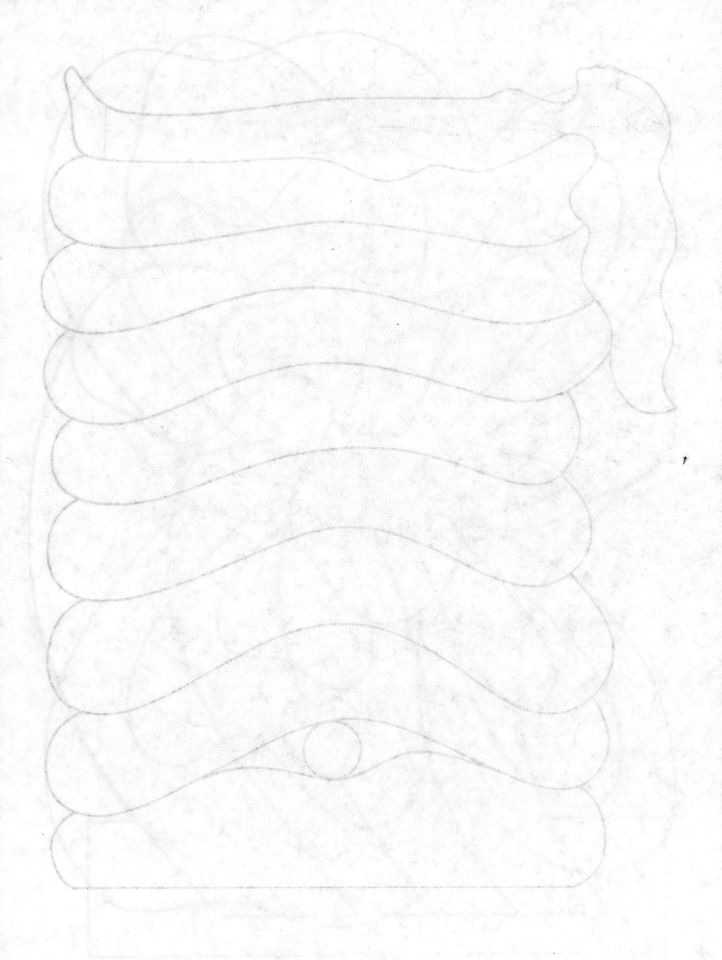

PLATE 2

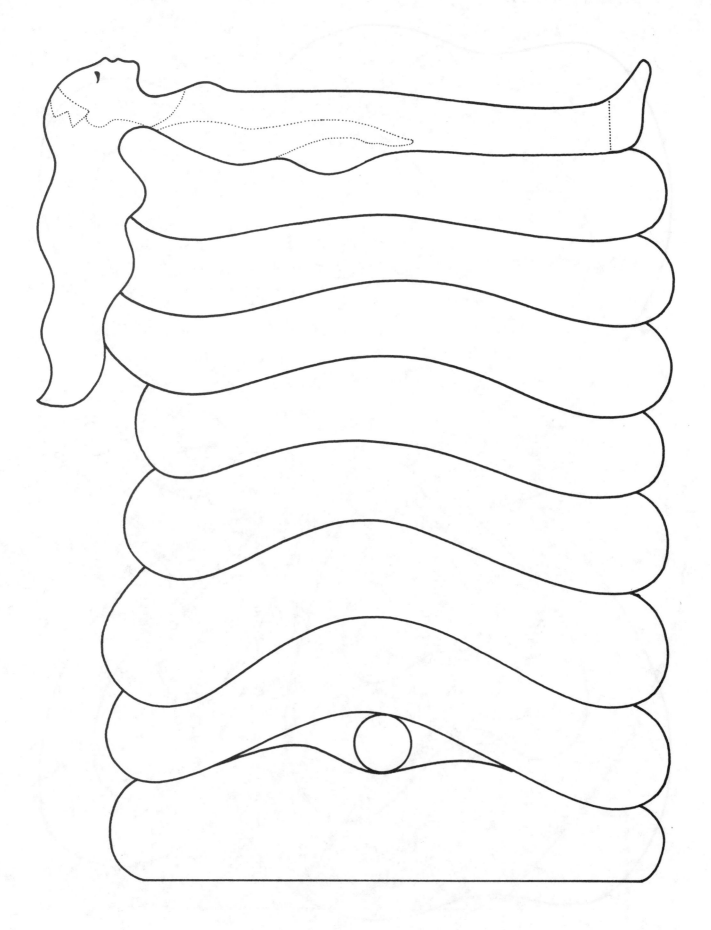

PLATE 2

PLATE 3

PLATE 4

PLATE 4

PLATE 5

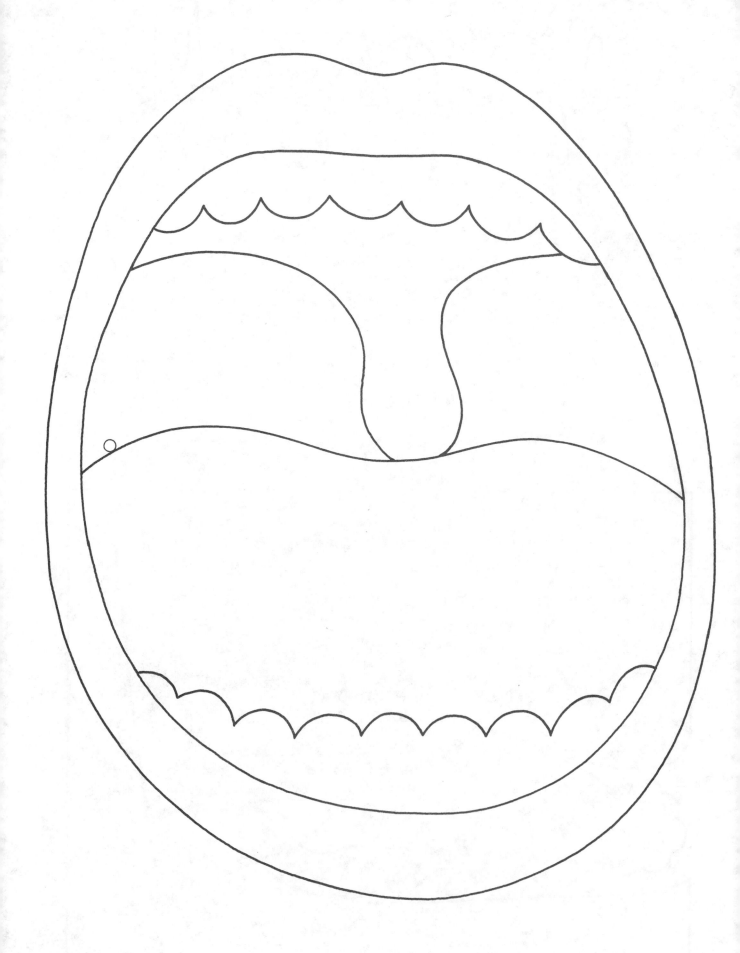

PLATE 6

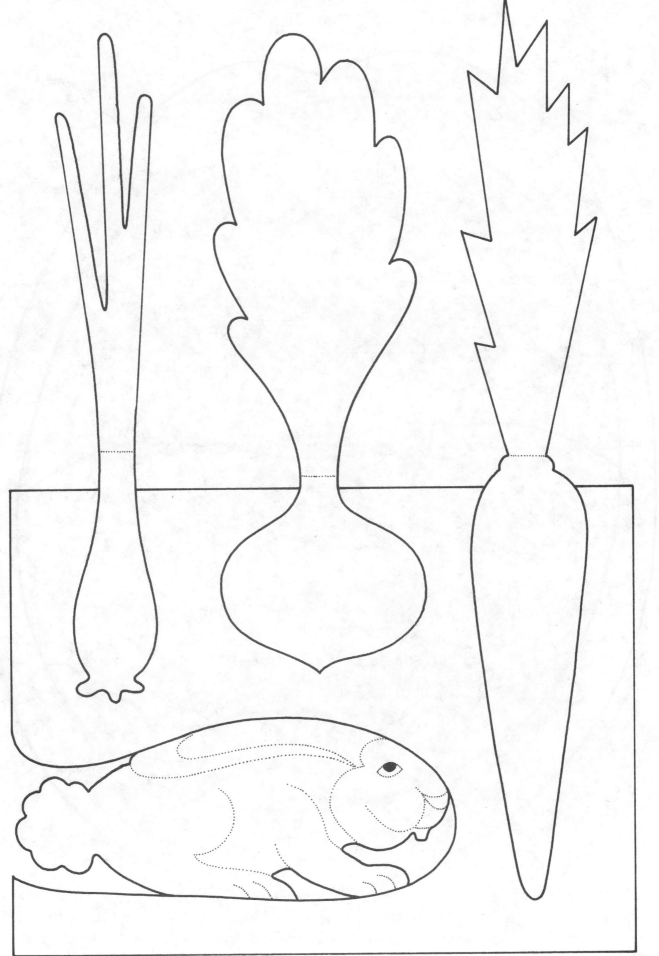

PLATE 7

PLATE 8

PLATE 9

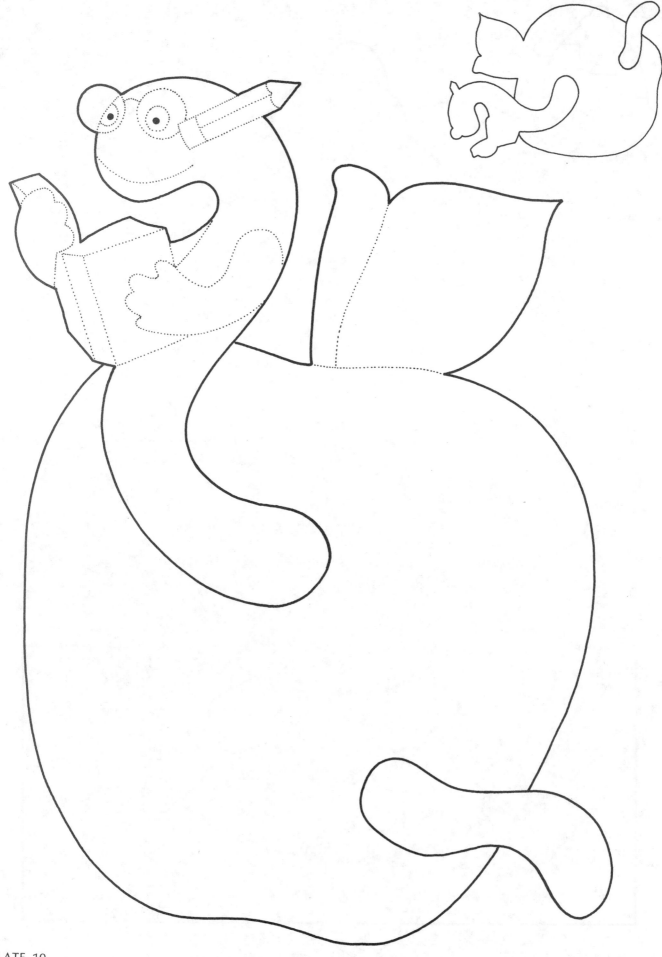

PLATE 10

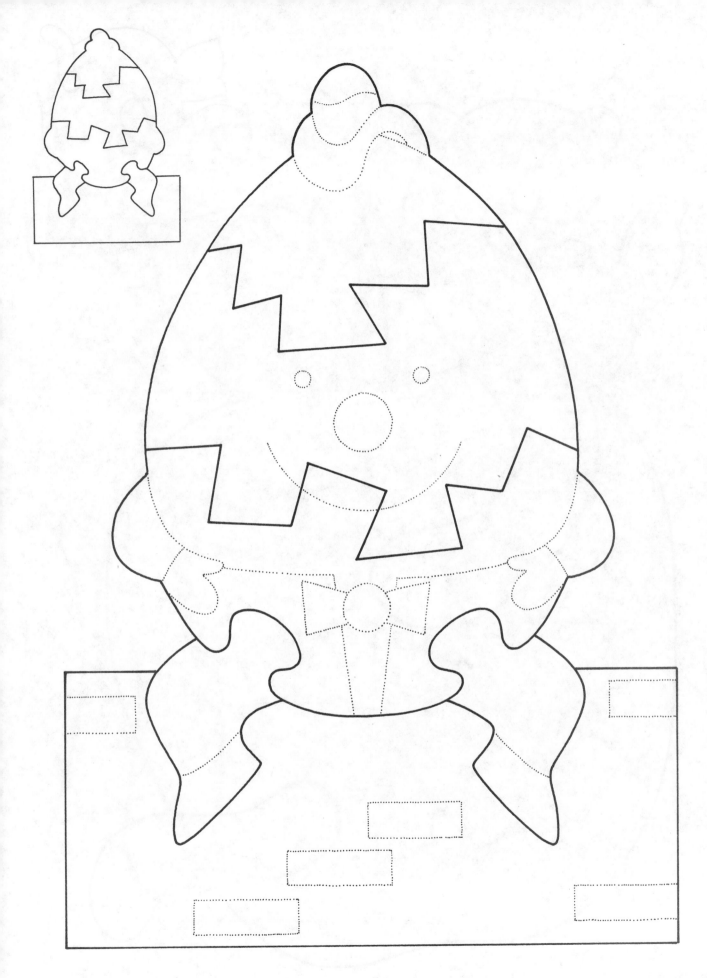

PLATE 11

PLATE 12

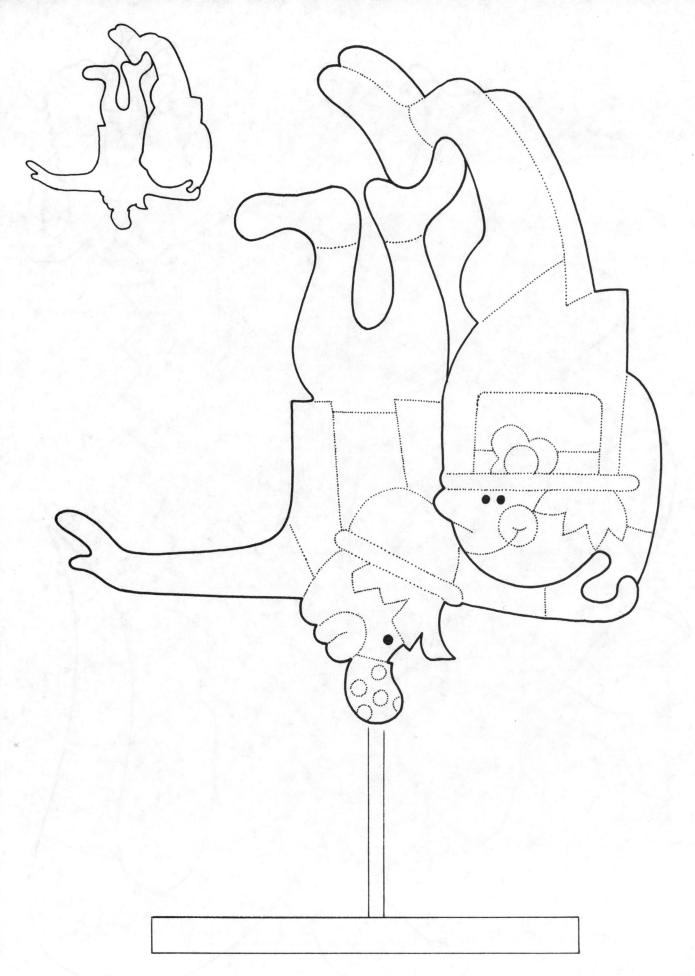

PLATE 13

PLATE 28

PLATE 29

PLATE 14

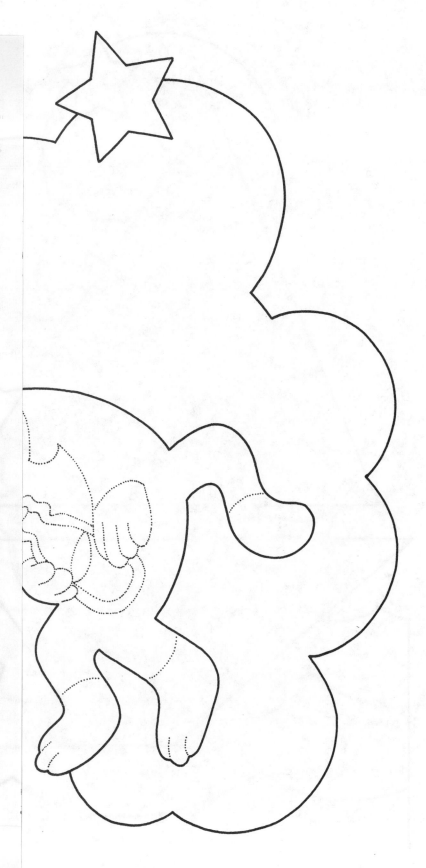

PLATE 15

PLATE 16

PLATE 16

PLATE 17

PLATE 18

PLATE 18

PLATE 19

PLATE 30

PLATE 20

PLATE 21

PLATE 21

PLATE 22.

PLATE 22

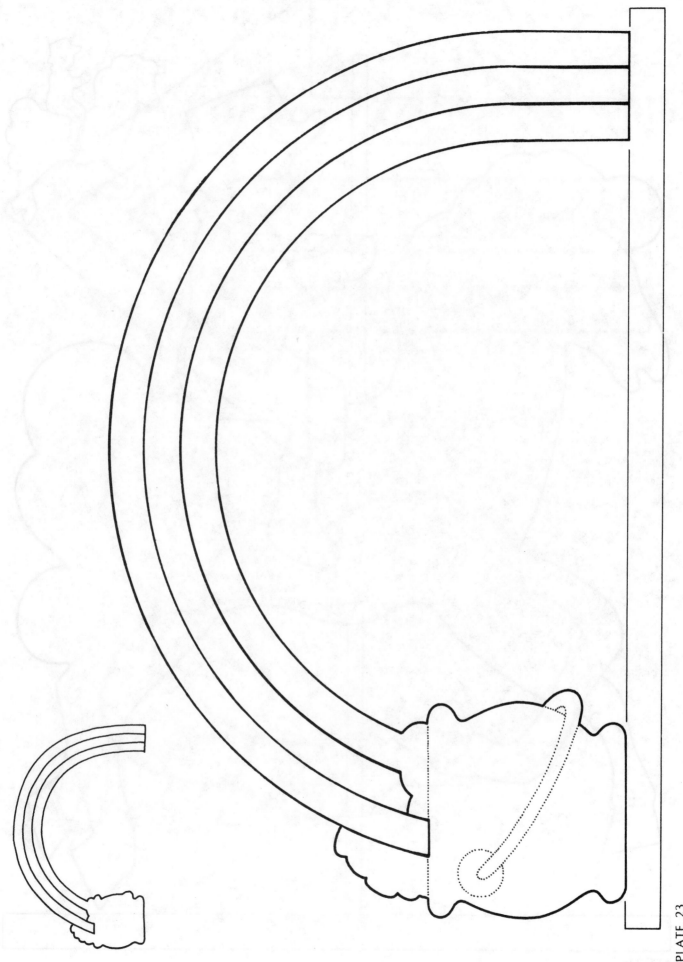

PLATE 23

PLATE 33

PLATE 24

PLATE 24

½" pine; the others can be cut from either ½" or ¾" pine.

2. Following the directions given below, iron the transfer pattern onto the wood.

3. Following the heavy lines, carefully cut out the figure and divide the pieces. In order to cut the toy made from plate 6, you will need to drill a small hole in the mouth to make room for the saw blade. The placement of this hole is indicated by the small circle on the transfer pattern.

4. Sand the rough edges very gently.

5. Using the color illustrations and the dotted lines as guides, paint the figure. The larger areas should be painted first; smaller areas can be painted over the large areas after the paint dries. Tiny areas such as eyes and eyelashes can be added with a marking pen. If you prefer using markers for the entire toy, be sure to use a permanent marker. Test the markers by applying the colors to a piece of scrap wood and then holding the wood under water after the marker has dried. If the color runs, the marker is not permanent.

TRANSFERRING THE PATTERNS

Before beginning any project it is a good idea to test your iron, the wood and the evenness of your hand pressure. Cut out one of the small drawings and follow the directions below for transferring. Since these transfer patterns are permanent, make certain that your test pattern is done on a piece of scrap wood. If the ink transferred well, you can proceed; if not, adjust either the heat or the length of time.

1. Use a dry iron set at the hottest temperature.

2. Place the piece of wood on a solid surface.

3. Remove the page (or cut out the motif), allowing a margin around the edges. With two or three pieces of tape or tacks through the margins attach the transfer to the wood with the printed side down. Protect the iron by placing a sheet of tissue paper between the transfer and the iron.

4. Place the heated iron on a part of the transfer and press down for approximately 10 seconds. The time required for transferring the design will increase as the transfer is reused. (You can usually get four or more transfers from each pattern.) Apply firm, even pressure to all parts of the design, being especially careful to get the outer edges, such as the tips of the pattern. Do not move the iron back and forth across the wood as this will cause the transfer to blur.

5. Carefully remove one fastener and lift the transfer paper to see whether the complete design is indicated on the wood. If not, replace the fastener and repeat the process. Do not remove all the fasteners until you are sure the entire design has been successfully transferred. Once the pattern has been removed it is almost impossible to register it to the wood again.

6. When you are satisfied that the transferring has been completed, remove the tacks or tape and the transfer pattern. You will want to save the transfer paper to use as a check on the design and for additional transfers if you wish to make another copy of the toy. If the design is not clear enough, you can reinforce vague areas with a pencil.

If you do not want to use an iron for transferring these designs, the patterns can be used for tracing the design onto the board. Put a piece of tracing paper over the uninked side of the transfer and trace the design. Put aside the original transfer paper and tack the tracing paper on the board. Slip a piece of carbon paper, color-side down, between the board and the tracing; do not tack the carbon. With a hard, even pressure trace a few lines with a pencil, stylus or similar tool. Raise one corner of the tracing and the carbon to check the impression. If the results are too faint, apply more pressure; if too heavy, less pressure. After adjusting the impression, trace the entire design and then remove the carbon and carefully remove one tack to see whether the design is intact on the board *before removing the pattern*. Be especially careful to differentiate between the cutting lines and the painting lines.

DO NOT GIVE PAINTED TOYS TO YOUNG CHILDREN WHO HAVE A TENDENCY TO PUT THINGS IN THEIR MOUTHS.

DOVER BOOKS ON
WOODWORKING AND CARVING

CARVING TROPICAL FISH, Anthony Hillman. (27094-7) $6.95

MAKING AUTHENTIC SHAKER FURNITURE, John G. Shea. (27003-3) $11.95

CARVING BIRDS OF PREY, Anthony Hillman. (27305-9) $6.95

HOW TO BUILD WOODEN BOATS, Edwin Monk. (27313-X) $7.95

MAKING AUTHENTIC PENNSYLVANIA DUTCH FURNITURE, John G. Shea.
    (27227-3) $12.95

EASY-TO-MAKE BIRD FEEDERS FOR WOODWORKERS, Scott D. Campbell.
    (25847-5) $2.95

THE BUILT-UP SHIP MODEL, Charles G. Davis. (26174-3) $5.95

CARVING DECORATIVE EAGLES, Anthony Hillman. (25976-5) $6.95

CARVING FAMOUS ANTIQUE BIRD DECOYS, Anthony Hillman.
    (25799-1) $6.95

CARVING POPULAR BIRDS, Anthony Hillman. (26136-0) $6.95

PAINTING POPULAR BIRD CARVINGS, Anthony Hillman. (26248-0) $5.95

PAINTING POPULAR DUCK DECOYS, Anthony Hillman. (26100-X) $5.95

WOODTURNING, Klaus Pracht. (Available in United States and Canada
    only). (25887-4) $22.95

MAKING ANIMAL PULLTOYS, Ed Sibbett, Jr. (26249-9) $3.50

THE BIG BOOK OF WHITTLING AND WOODCARVING, E. J. Tangerman.
    (26171-9) $12.95

THE BEGINNER'S HANDBOOK OF WOODCARVING, Charles Beiderman and
    William Johnston. (25687-1) $7.95

THE SHIP MODEL BUILDER'S ASSISTANT, Charles Davis. (25584-0) $7.95

SHIP MODELS: HOW TO BUILD THEM, Charles G. Davis. (25170-5) $6.95

CARVING CLASSIC SWAN AND GOOSE DECOYS, Anthony Hillman.
    (25522-0) $6.95

CARVING EARLY AMERICAN WEATHERVANES, Anthony Hillman.
    (25223-X) $5.95

CARVING MINIATURE DUCK DECOYS, Anthony Hillman. (24936-0) $6.95

PAINTING SHOREBIRD DECOYS, Anthony Hillman. (25349-X) $5.95

PAINTING SONGBIRD CARVINGS, Anthony Hillman. (25580-8) $5.95

EASY CARPENTRY PROJECTS FOR CHILDREN, Jerome Leavitt.
    (25057-1) $3.95

Paperbound unless otherwise indicated. Prices subject to change
without notice. Available at your book dealer or write for free catalogues
to Dept. 23, Dover Publications, Inc., 31 East 2nd Street, Mineola, N.Y.
11501. Please indicate field of interest. Each year Dover publishes over
200 books on fine art, music, crafts and needlework, antiques,
languages, literature, children's books, chess, cookery, nature,
anthropology, science, mathematics, and other areas.

Manufactured in the U.S.A.